THE POWER OF INTUITION

TRUST YOUR INNER WISDOM

Published by Hinkler Pty Ltd
45–55 Fairchild Street
Heatherton Victoria 3202 Australia
www.hinkler.com

© Hinkler Pty Ltd 2021, 2022

Author: Angela Martin
Internal design: Lisa Robertson
Cover design: Maria Daley and Hinkler Studio

Images © Shutterstock.com

All rights reserved. No part of this publication may be reproduced, stored in a retrieval system, or transmitted in any way or by any means electronic, mechanical, photocopying, recording or otherwise, without the prior written permission of Hinkler Pty Ltd.

ISBN: 978 1 4889 4751 3

Printed and bound in Malaysia

THE POWER OF
INTUITION

TRUST YOUR INNER WISDOM

Angela Martin

> This idea of submission to deep intuition appears to be exactly what many successful people in a wide variety of fields have come to adopt.

Willis Harman, author

CONTENTS

Introduction 6

Intuition 8
What is it? 8
How does it work? 12
History of intuition 14
Childhood intuition 16
Nurturing children's
intuitive possibilities 16

Identifying intuition 20
Types of intuitive experience 20
Learning to pay attention 25
Watching out for synchronicities 26
Understanding your gut feelings........29
Intuitive intelligence 30
Women's intuition 34

Developing your intuition 38
Getting started 38
Awakening your intuition...................40
Sharpening your senses 42
Finding your intuitive state 46
Using fantasy, imagination
and dreams.......................................48
Images and symbols.........................50
Nurturing your intuition 52

Harnessing your intuition 56
Knowing what you want....................56
Using creative visualisation..............60
Asking the right questions 64
The art of interpretation 66
Intuition and reason together............68
Is it really intuition? 70

Intuition in action 72
Everyday intuition 72
Developing problem-solving
techniques.......................................76
Intuition on the job 78
Intuition in business 80
Intuition, medicine and healing.........84

The practice of intuition 86
Using objects to guide you................86
Your intuitive style 89
Tapping into creative sources...........92
What next?...................................... 94

Introduction

In these complex times, with life moving at a fast pace, everyone would like some guidance. We yearn for quick, easy answers to the difficult questions that face us each day. It would be convenient to know in an instant which way to turn, which path to take.

We can easily feel overwhelmed with information and confused by endless options – it can be comforting to turn to specialists and experts to show us the way. But asking others to make decisions for us can leave us feeling less competent than ever.

There is a way to regain a sense of control over our lives. By using our intuition, we can reclaim our own power; we can rely on our ability to make decisions for ourselves.

Intuition is knowledge that springs from an expanded state of awareness. It does not promise an easy answer in the blink of an eye, but it does always offer answers to questions we may have formulated either consciously or subconsciously.

Most of us use intuition in one way or another more frequently than we imagine. Sometimes we refer to it as 'a natural instinct' or 'a hunch' that would inform us if we would only listen carefully and take note. Sometimes we say 'it just feels right' or 'it sits well with me'. We have a sense that now is the time to move forwards or to hold back. These are all examples of practical intuition.

One of the reasons why so many shy away from practising the art of intuition is that it has long had the flavour of mysticism. Intangible and mysterious, it has been the province of the more eccentric. However, this attitude has been changing over the last few years as we become more and more aware of the importance of paying attention to both the rational and the intuitive.

Although the rational, which exists in the realm of the intellect, has long been given prominence in decision-making, we recognise now that the two types of consciousness are complementary modes of functioning. In other words, decisions are best made on the basis of an integration between the rational mind (sometimes in the past called 'the masculine mind') and the intuitive mind (sometimes in the past called 'the feminine mind').

In this book you will find out all you need to know to begin using practical intuition. Exercises are presented throughout the book to start you on your way. You will find out how to awaken your intuitive mind, how to tap into it and how to nurture it. You will learn how to recognise the 'voice' of your own intuition – intuition speaks to each of us in unique and personal ways. And you will also learn how to build your own individual dictionary of symbols; this will be an invaluable ongoing resource for you.

Intuition is a serious business, but it's also lots of fun. So, enjoy making your way through these pages, inviting new possibilities into your life by drawing on a gift that is available to each one of us.

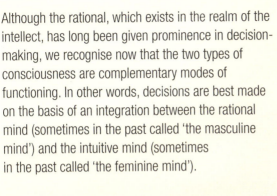

Intuition

What is it?

Take a few moments to reflect on what you understand by the term 'intuition'. Allow time for examples of intuitive experience of your own to float to the surface of your mind. Jot down ideas that come to you, words that seem to express your own definition of the term.

Intuition has long been considered an elusive concept, one with mystical connotations, and it is difficult to define. Ask your friends what they think intuition is and you might come up with a whole range of definitions. Here is a sample of responses to the question:

- 'Intuition is a quiet but firm inner voice.'
- 'It's like an animal instinct, an urge to move in a particular direction.'
- 'It is God's voice, speaking directly to me.'
- 'Intuition is a sort of impulse. But it doesn't mean you act impulsively.'
- 'It is a flash of insight that comes from nowhere.'
- 'Intuition is what comes to me in answer to my prayers.'
- 'It's the voice of my guardian angel guiding me.'
- 'It's a hunch, a sense that this is the way to go.'
- 'Intuition is a gut feeling. It happens without any effort from me.'
- 'It's knowing something clearly, without knowing how you came to know it.'

There are many different terms used here, but notice that at the heart of all these attempts at definition is the understanding that intuition involves no conscious use of the reasoning mind. It is a 'knowing' and it expresses itself to each of us in many ways.

> The intellect has little to do on the road to discovery. There comes a leap in consciousness, call it intuition or what you will, and the solution comes to you, and you don't know how or why.

Albert Einstein, physicist

Instinct, gut feelings and intuition

The term 'instinct' is used often as a synonym for intuition. Intuition is very much allied to instinct, which refers to a natural response to a stimulus. For example, the 'fight or flight' feeling humans experience is allied to animal instinct. Instinct is a natural response involving the senses. Intuition, however, combines instinct with a cognitive element. People who use their intuition often may well talk about 'acting instinctively' because their intuition may be so highly developed and their use of it so frequent that they respond to its call spontaneously and immediately.

'A gut feeling' refers to a body response that may not necessarily be located in the gut area. Perhaps the term is used because the gut is the site of one of the most basic of bodily processes – the digestion and absorption of food. Certainly, in our culture, 'having a gut feeling' is often used interchangeably with 'having an intuition'.

Sixth sense and other psychic phenomena

Intuition is also referred to as 'the sixth sense', defined in Merriam-Webster's dictionary as 'a power of perception like but not one of the five senses: a keen intuitive power'. This is certainly how those who trust their intuition and regard it as a guiding principle in their life feel about it.

The term 'sixth sense' has come to be strongly associated with psychic phenomena. But while intuition is available to every individual, other 'abilities', such as the facility for telepathy or psychic vision, are specialised areas within the broad field of intuition and do not seem to be available to all of us.

How does it work?

The Latin roots of the word intuition mean 'to regard inwards'. This gives a strong clue as to what is involved. Intuition arises from within, even though outer elements – such as objects or other people or events – may be present and play a part.

Those who use intuition regularly in their lives, and those who help others to access it, emphasise the importance of developing inner quiet. This involves techniques to silence the chattering mind. Because the mind tends to analyse, rationalise, explain and interpret, it can be both interfering and invasive when we allow it too much control. One way of understanding how intuition works is to imagine quietening the mind so that other parts of ourselves, parts which are usually silenced and ignored, can communicate another sort of knowledge. The paradox in trying to explain how intuition works is that we try to do it using language, a linear way of communicating. However, intuition is non-linear. To understand this, consider the times you've had a hunch or a gut feeling. It would not have come as a set of instructions or rules, and probably did not come in terms of language at all. It would more likely have come as a body sense, or a flash, or an image or a sound.

How intuition works is not entirely understood, although there are various ideas about it. These will become more apparent as you work your way through this book. The exercises will provide some understanding of how it works, and continued practice will further reveal some of its mysteries.

How can intuition work for you?

An early step towards developing and harnessing your intuition is to acknowledge that there is much about how the universe works that your mind can't comprehend. When you become open to possibilities, your consciousness will expand, and your intuition will grow accordingly. In the following pages, you'll learn how to awaken your intuition and how to find your own intuitive state. By developing your ability to access your intuition through the practical applications in this book, you'll be shown how to define what it is that you want. You'll find out how to encourage your intuition and reason to work together in a way that opens a new world to you.

Intuition can work for you in the everyday decisions you have to make, in the guidance you want when life's path is not clear; it can work for you when you need to solve problems, and when you feel your creativity is stifled. Whatever your concern, whether large or small, you'll find your intuition will guide you in an intelligent and satisfying way.

History of intuition

> *At one time, and even today in some cultures, people faced with tough decisions consulted astrologers or psychics. They could receive guidance from diviners, who read the sound of thunder, the entrails of animals, or the flights of birds for meaning and insight.*
> **THOMAS MOORE, PSYCHOTHERAPIST AND WRITER**

The history of intuition is as long as the history of humankind. Intuitive powers are firmly established, human beings in most communities were more open to a world not hallmarks of our species. The evolution in communication and the innovative use of was central to the process of living.

The discovery and development of devices that were central to various early civilisations could be attributed to the power of intuition.

Paradigm shifts are often associated with the intuitive process. A paradigm is a belief system, a particular way of seeing, so a paradigm shift is a total change in the way of seeing things, and it involves not just a step or two, but a quantum leap in terms of understanding. Paradigm shifts, such as the invention of the wheel and the theory that the world is round, may well have been fuelled by hunches, gut feelings or intuition.

Back in the 5th century BC, the Greek philosopher Hippocrates, known as the father of medicine, wrote about the value of intuition, which he called 'instinct', and the importance of heeding it. He warned that 'cold reason' can obscure our inner vision, which 'must never be disdained'. Our very first remedies, he recorded, were due to instinct, and instinct alone.

Through the ages, instances of instinct or intuition in action have been reported, most notably in the artistic and scientific fields. Remember Archimedes from Syracuse, in Greece, the 3rd century BC mathematician, crying 'Eureka' when he discovered in the bath the basis of what became his famous principle: that a body immersed in a fluid is buoyed up by a source that is equal to the weight of the fluid displaced? And Albert Einstein, who so profoundly influenced science in many fields, was a great believer in intuition, which he credited for many of his own inspirations.

> *A hunch is creativity trying to tell you something.*
> FRANK CAPRA, FILM DIRECTOR

It has long been understood and accepted that painters and artists and composers and writers and film-makers rely greatly on instinct or intuition when producing their works. They do not rely only on logical or sequential methods, but also trust their intuitive powers to provide them with creative ideas and approaches central to their work.

Our emphasis on using a logical, rational, sequential approach to learn about the world and ourselves, epitomised by scientific experiments and data, is a relatively recent phenomenon. Up until a few centuries ago, when this mechanistic approach became firmly established, human beings in most communities were more open to a world not limited by 'proven facts' and to matters driven by logic. Intuition, in its various guises, was central to the process of living. A continuing desire and search for understanding about how we work (and for ways to cure illnesses) has led research into the brain and its processes. The discovery of 'the triune brain', discussed later in the book, has led the way in explaining where intuition might originate and how it can be integrated with logic and reasoning. This discovery is merely the latest in the history of intuition; no doubt there is still much to discover about its origins.

Childhood intuition

> *Sometimes I just know things, and Mum says 'How do you know that?'*
> *I don't know how I know. I just do. And my friend Jasmine does too.*
> ISABELLE, AGED 6

Do children have intuition? Some people would argue that children are highly intuitive, and that adults steeped in a culture of logic and reason don't recognise this and may even actively work against it. How?

By imposing too much adult direction and structure, not allowing enough 'quiet time' for children, and rejecting their comments as 'silly' or 'not real'.

For adults who want to encourage and nurture children's intuitive powers, the best approach is to stand back and allow them to unfold at their own pace and in their own way, giving plenty of opportunities for them to grow in as whole a way as possible. That means honouring the role of logic and reason along with the role of intuition.

Nurturing children's intuitive possibilities

Children's intuition can be developed and nurtured by;

- Allowing them time to unwind from the day;
- Preventing too much sensory input;
- Encouraging their imagination;
- Delighting in their flights of fancy;
- Listening to their stories;
- Paying attention when they express concerns or fears.

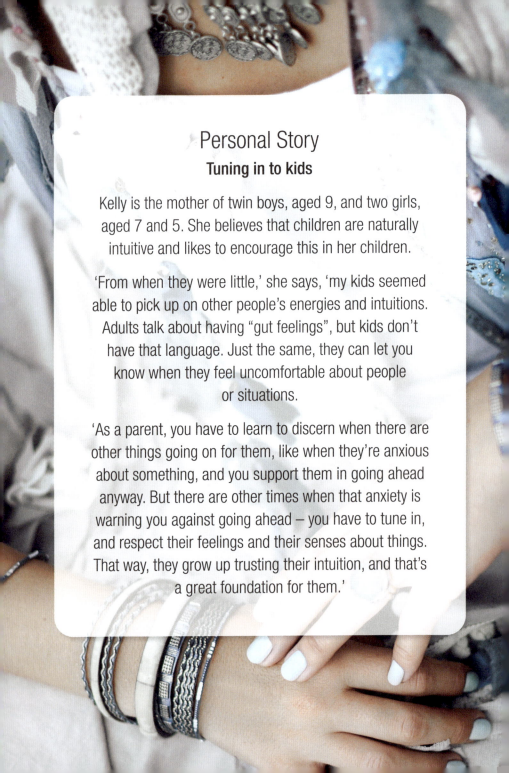

Personal Story
Tuning in to kids

Kelly is the mother of twin boys, aged 9, and two girls, aged 7 and 5. She believes that children are naturally intuitive and likes to encourage this in her children.

'From when they were little,' she says, 'my kids seemed able to pick up on other people's energies and intuitions. Adults talk about having "gut feelings", but kids don't have that language. Just the same, they can let you know when they feel uncomfortable about people or situations.

'As a parent, you have to learn to discern when there are other things going on for them, like when they're anxious about something, and you support them in going ahead anyway. But there are other times when that anxiety is warning you against going ahead — you have to tune in, and respect their feelings and their senses about things. That way, they grow up trusting their intuition, and that's a great foundation for them.'

> When things are coasting along smoothly, we don't need guidance. The sudden flashes of intuition and dreams we have in our darkest hours, however, are capable of renewing our lives, changing our course, and mending a broken spirit.

Joan Borysenko,
psychoneuroimmunologist

Identifying intuition

Types of intuitive experience

I have had my solutions for a long time, but I do not yet know how I am to arrive at them.
CARL GAUSS, MATHEMATICIAN

One of the difficult things about pinning down definitions of intuition is that it can be given expression, or surface, in a number of different ways. For example, someone who has been working on a problem for some time may find that one day, almost out of the blue, the solution will appear. There are numbers of reports of scientists and artists who immerse themselves in a subject area, trying hard to find a way through, only to arrive at a resolution at a later date, when they least expected it.

This phenomenon has been described as 'intuition with precedent' and it is believed to arise after an incubation period. The conscious mind goes on being distracted by other things, thinks about what is at hand, moves on to other problems. But just underneath, below the level of consciousness, a lot of work is going on. Ideas are swirling this way and that, matching up here and there, filling the space and preparing to be 'born'.

Another type of intuition is that without precedent, when a hunch or gut feeling arises with no prior experience. It happens, for example, when you suddenly sense that you should take this particular course of action, or when you have a gut feeling that you can either totally trust (or not trust!) a person you have just met.

To get to know the sort of intuitive experiences you tend to have, try the following exercise. It will help you identify those moments when you suddenly have an answer to a problem you've been mulling over, and those moments when you suddenly have a hunch that appears out of nowhere.

Exercise — Getting to know your intuition

Take some time to reflect on your past experiences of intuition. Relax, let yourself drift back to those intuitive times …

- Have you ever had an 'aha' experience after trying to arrive at a solution?
- Have you ever had a hunch about something?
- Is there another type of intuition that you have experienced?

Personal Stories
Emerging insights

Paul, a young man who is keen to develop his intuitive powers, comments that he often has intuitive thoughts after he has been working hard mentally. 'It's when I walk away from my study and take a shower, for instance, or take a stroll, or poke around in the garden, that all sorts of intuitive insights will emerge.

'It's as though my conscious mind has been taking over, grinding itself down in logic and reason, and then, when it has a chance, my subconscious reasserts itself with its wonderfully rich ideas and connections.'

Learning to pay attention

The notion of paying attention is usually associated with schooldays, when you were expected to bring your mind to the task at hand. You may wish that you'd had time to daydream more back then, but while daydreaming has an important part to play in life, paying attention is important too. Believe it or not, few people pay much attention to what is going on around them. Think about it.

- Do you move through your days with your focus on the next step, or even the fiftieth step ahead?
- Do you let your mind rake up past events over and over again?
- Does your mind fly off in all directions, with your crazy thoughts leading you on a merry chase?

It can be difficult to really be here in the present, taking full notice of your current experience. However, intuition relies on attention. How else will you recognise its message?

Learning to pay attention will repay you in many ways. For example:

- You will begin to notice things with a new appreciation.
- You will see what you haven't seen before.
- You will begin making connections between events that have seemed entirely unconnected.
- You will start to see purpose and meaning, because although you may not understand what is happening, somehow everything makes more sense.

Start to bring your full awareness to every activity in your day – when getting out of bed or preparing your meals, when making a phone call or paying your bills, when sitting in the sunshine or walking your dog. Be there fully, notice everything. Be in the moment. Be alive to your everyday life.

When you bring your focus to what you are doing in the present moment, paying attention to the details, you will more easily identify your intuition.

Watching out for synchronicities

There is no such thing as chance; and that which seems to us blind accident actually stems from the deepest source of all.
FRIEDRICH VON SCHILLER, WRITER AND PHILOSOPHER

Once you are paying more attention to the world around you, your consciousness will expand. In other words, all types of things that once escaped your notice will now be more apparent to you.

You might begin to notice an increasing number of coincidences, sometimes referred to as 'synchronicities'. The psychoanalyst Carl Jung coined the term 'synchronicity' for an event that may seem coincidental but has deeper meaning. That is, such events remind us of the inherent harmony in the world, and they present us with opportunities to look more carefully at what we might otherwise dismiss as only coincidence.

Have you ever:

- Thought about someone and then bumped into them soon after?
- Reminded yourself to call an old friend, and they call you first?
- Met up 'accidentally' with someone you know in the most unlikely place?
- Had a question in your mind only to have it answered unexpectedly when you switch on the radio or television?
- Tried to remember a particular detail and then had it 'arrive' in your mind in what seems like the oddest way?

These are all synchronicities in action. In fact, in the Vedic tradition (the sacred roots of Hinduism), those who are in the process of enlightenment become aware of an increasing number of synchronicities in their life.

When you pay attention, when you are alert and open to possibilities, you may find that in those strange and wonderful coincidences lie clues to a new understanding, or a new direction, or a new piece of knowledge. It is through synchronicities that intuition can make itself known. Be awake to them.

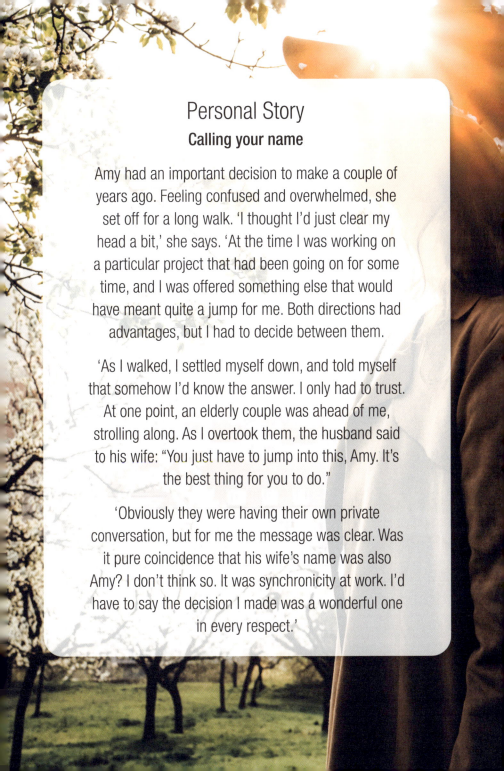

Personal Story
Calling your name

Amy had an important decision to make a couple of years ago. Feeling confused and overwhelmed, she set off for a long walk. 'I thought I'd just clear my head a bit,' she says. 'At the time I was working on a particular project that had been going on for some time, and I was offered something else that would have meant quite a jump for me. Both directions had advantages, but I had to decide between them.

'As I walked, I settled myself down, and told myself that somehow I'd know the answer. I only had to trust. At one point, an elderly couple was ahead of me, strolling along. As I overtook them, the husband said to his wife: "You just have to jump into this, Amy. It's the best thing for you to do."

'Obviously they were having their own private conversation, but for me the message was clear. Was it pure coincidence that his wife's name was also Amy? I don't think so. It was synchronicity at work. I'd have to say the decision I made was a wonderful one in every respect.'

Understanding your gut feelings

Despite its name, a gut feeling can occur anywhere in your body. While for some people it is in the gut area, others report that they have tingling fingers, for example, or that their chest grows a little tight.

There are various theories put forward to explain what is happening physiologically and biochemically in your body when you have a gut feeling. What is most helpful to you in developing and harnessing practical intuition is to increase your self-awareness and improve your ability to observe yourself. The following exercise, *Identify your gut feelings*, will help you with that.

The more attention you give to building this skill, the more easily you will be able to identify your gut feelings and listen to what they are telling you.

Exercise — Identify your gut feelings

This exercise will sharpen your skills in observing yourself and your responses, an essential step in developing your intuition.

- Settle down, get comfortable, relax, and then …
- Remember a time when you had a gut feeling about something. Allow yourself to go back to that instance, and reflect on these questions. You may want to record your responses in a journal:
  » Where were you?
  » How did you look?
  » How did your body feel?
  » What were your emotions?
  » What did this gut feeling have in common with other gut feelings you've had?
- Practise this exercise regularly to better develop your skills. And next time you actually have a gut feeling, sit down with it and go through the same exercise, jotting down your responses for the future reference.

Intuitive intelligence

It may come as a surprise to you to know that intuition is considered an intellectual skill. The idea that being intuitive is a natural state of the brain, and that using it to get information is perfectly valid, cuts across those who criticise intuition as being in the realm of fantasy only.

The research of neurophysiologist Dr Paul MacLean has revealed a collection of separate bits in the brain. Dr MacLean coined the term 'triune brain' to explain the total brain system. His diagram of the brain illustrates the placement of what he describes as our three brains: the reptilian (or primal) brain, the limbic system, and the neocortex, which itself is divided into two hemispheres (sometimes known as the left and right brains).

You find out about the world through all these systems. For example:

- The primitive brain (or reptilian brain) is the earliest in terms of evolution. It controls our automatic and instinctual responses, such as the fight or flight response.
- The limbic system (or limbic lobes) is also known as the mammalian brain, and is the most chemically active of the brains. It is the centre of our emotional responses.
- The neocortex surrounds the mammalian brain. Our logical thinking springs from here, as does our voluntary muscle control.

The triune brain

- neocortex
- limbic system
- primitive brain

The functions of the two hemispheres

Left hemisphere

- Centre of language
- Picks up information in steps/reduces facts to simplest elements
- Uses logic
- Engages in sequential reasoning
- Processes data verbally

Right hemisphere

- Non-verbal
- Picks up information as a whole/sees the big picture
- Creates meaning
- Centre of creativity and intuition
- Sends non-verbal data

From the front, the brain resembles a large walnut. Down the centre runs a notch, separating the brain into two hemispheres. Because of the way the neurons (nerve cells) run through the brain from the body, the left part of the brain controls the right side of the body and the right part controls the left side. The left and right hemispheres are joined by a bridge known as the corpus callosum, which contains more than 200 million nerve fibres. The right hemisphere has no language, but one theory is that it 'confers with' the limbic system, the centre of our emotions, when it takes in information. Perhaps this is why we talk about having 'a sense' about something or 'a gut feeling'.

Intuitive thought has not had, at least in Western cultures in the last two centuries, the respect that logical, rational thought has enjoyed. Consequently, you may find that, like most people, you favour logic and rational thought. However, researchers into 'the whole-brain approach' (engaging both hemispheres of the brain) emphasise the importance of honouring intuitive intelligence, and point out the importance of allowing the rational and the intuitive brains to work together – when they do work together, you'll be taking in more information. And you can train your left and right hemispheres to complement each other: the right can help provide the data, and the left can interpret and verbalise it so that you can check out your hunches.

Women's intuition

*The deepest experience of the creator is feminine,
for it is experience of receiving and bearing.*
RAINER MARIA RILKE, POET AND AUTHOR

The term 'women's intuition' is a common one, used by both men and women to explain the suggestions women make that are based on gut feelings and senses.

Are women more intuitive than men? One theory comes from the world of physiology. Research indicates that in women, the cross section of the corpus callosum (the bridge between the two hemispheres of the neocortex) is larger across all fibres. This means that the interaction between the two hemispheres is faster and easier. In other words, women can combine the logic of the left hemisphere and the intuition of the right hemisphere more easily. What's more, these neural fibres actually mature several years earlier in girls than in boys, so girls have some time to practise more integrated thinking.

All the same, males do have natural intuitive abilities, and, like women, they can work at developing them, adding 'muscle' to them, and harnessing them for practical use. Until now, 'women's intuition' has referred to the tendency in women to have more highly developed intuitive skills. But as intuition gains increasing recognition and respect, many men who have relied more heavily on their powers of logic may well embrace their own intuitive powers.

> Intuition is the treasure of a woman's psyche.

Clarissa Pinkola Estés,
Jungian analyst and author

Personal Stories

The sacred thing

Susie says: 'My intuition is so important to me, both personally and professionally. I grew up in a family of three daughters, and both my sisters are also strongly intuitive. All of us found [that] during our pregnancies we were even more intuitive than usual. I think it's because you become more internal, you listen more, you are more receptive, when you are pregnant. For me, intuition is a sacred thing, something to honour and respect.'

Something special

'I don't like the idea of women's intuition,' says teacher Steve. 'It makes as much sense as talking about "men's intellect", which is of course ridiculous. Both men and women have intellect. 'And I feel strongly that both men and women have intuition. Talking about "women's intuition" makes it sound like something special that only half the population enjoys. I have gut feelings. I have hunches. I have intuition. And men should be encouraged to use their intuition, rather than being made to feel they are missing out on something so valuable.'

Developing your intuition

Getting started

You've decided to develop your intuition, so have some fun organising a few basics. You may not have to go shopping – the items on the list below may be things you already have. Whether or not you make purchases to get started, choose what brings you delight. Your intuition loves you to enjoy yourself, so let go and do just that.

Your intuition kit (everything is optional):

- A journal;
- Coloured pencils;
- An assortment of pens;
- Glue;
- Images/pictures/magazine cuttings;
- A tape recorder.

- The journal will be used to record your responses to the exercises that are described in this book, and to build your own dictionary of intuitive vocabulary (more on page 51). You may want to record your dreams, too, if you don't have a dream journal already. And the journal is a good place to note down those synchronicities that hold intuitive clues. A large exercise book makes a fine journal – cover it and decorate it to your taste, and keep it handy.
- You may like to use coloured pencils for recording your hunches and your dreams, for noting your synchronicities and for building your dictionary of symbols, for decorative borders and inspiring doodles. The colours you use will help spark your creativity and engage your intuitive powers.
- Use your favoured pens, too, and keep in mind that as you write, you don't have to keep things sequential. For example, if you're doing some jotting rather than straight prose, try writing this way and that all over the page. Again, it stimulates your creativity.

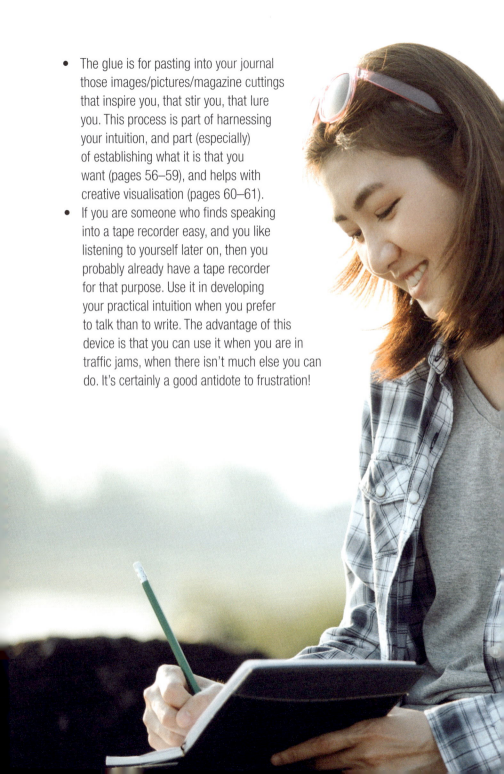

- The glue is for pasting into your journal those images/pictures/magazine cuttings that inspire you, that stir you, that lure you. This process is part of harnessing your intuition, and part (especially) of establishing what it is that you want (pages 56–59), and helps with creative visualisation (pages 60–61).
- If you are someone who finds speaking into a tape recorder easy, and you like listening to yourself later on, then you probably already have a tape recorder for that purpose. Use it in developing your practical intuition when you prefer to talk than to write. The advantage of this device is that you can use it when you are in traffic jams, when there isn't much else you can do. It's certainly a good antidote to frustration!

Awakening your intuition

Your intuition is always available to you, but it could be that it is taking a temporary nap to cope with the cacophony and frenzy of your everyday mind. If that's the case, then you'll need to take steps to awaken it, to let it know that you are ready and willing to listen well to it.

The quiet truth of our lives is always waiting, and it often communicates itself in subtle messages. It's up to each of us to prepare ourselves to hear it. You can do this by:

- Slowing down;
- Stilling your mind;
- Learning to be comfortable with silence;
- Focusing on the first faint whispers of intuition.

As you move into slowness and silence, you'll feel softer and more receptive. This is the place that intuition loves best. To help you get there, practise the following exercises: *Relax your ever-active mind* (page 41) and *Listen deeply* (page 55).

To begin, read them through a few times so that you really understand each step of each process, and then practise them as regularly as you can – at least once a day is ideal. In time you'll find that you will be able to do the exercises spontaneously, relaxing your mind and listening fully in a matter of moments.

Exercise — Relax your ever-active mind

- Sit comfortably, and close your eyes.

- Notice your mind darting here and there, flitting from topic to topic, issue to issue, always on the go, judging, analysing, commenting, unable to stop. Rather than resisting it, focus on its busy-ness.

- Go right in there, feeling its tension, its need to get things right, its need to comment on everything. Be inside that mind, that chattering, ever-moving mind. Feel its frenzy. Sink into that mind.

- Allow yourself to be there for a while, and then imagine the chaos and noise subsiding. Gradually, gradually, it is slowing down. Gradually it is relaxing, resting, softening. Be there with your softening mind.

- Feel it let go. Feel it let the tension ooze away. Feel your mind slowing in its tracks.

- Open your eyes and sit quietly. Let that quietened mind sit still with you. Keep breathing. Ignore the chatter that might start up again. Sit with your still mind.

Sharpening your senses

The moment one gives close attention to anything, even a blade of grass, it becomes a mysterious, awesome, indescribably magnificent world in itself.
HENRY MILLER, AUTHOR

Like many people, you may be leading a very busy life, rushing from one activity to another and tending to many responsibilities. When you lead such a rushed existence, you tend to be focused on what you need to do tomorrow, and what you should have done yesterday: in other words, on anything but the present.

Remember the saying 'stop and smell the roses'? The point of it is that when you are busy, you stop feeding your senses. Who has time to look at beautiful things? To smell delicious aromas? To delight in sensuous touch? To listen to anything other than the demands of the ticking clock?

And when your senses are not fed, they become blunted. In this state of impoverishment, you are likely to miss intuitive possibilities, because it is through the senses that intuition is most likely to express itself.

This book gives you the opportunity to sharpen your senses. The exercise *Notice the detail* (page 44) will guide you through the senses, allowing you to focus on each one in turn. Sharpened senses mean that you are more alive, not only physically, but in other dimensions as well. And when you are physically more alert and responsive, you'll recognise those gut feelings and hunches more easily.

Exercise — Notice the detail

Sit in a comfortable position, preferably in a favourite spot. It could be outdoors, in your own garden or courtyard, or it could be indoors, either in your own home or in a café. In fact, once you've tried this particular exercise, you can take it anywhere you like. You'll find yourself noticing the detail in an airport lounge, in a waiting room, in a line for the bus or in the supermarket. Any place is good enough when it comes to sharpening your senses.

- Now use your eyes to look around, and choose just one detail from what you see. It could be the colour of a chair or the shape of a photo frame. It could be the petal of a flower, or it could be a brick. It really doesn't matter what it is. Focus on the detail, noticing all that you can. Notice the colour, the texture, the shape, the little bits that you ordinarily would not see. Let your eyes linger there for some time, taking in every detail.

- Now sharpen your hearing. Tune in to the sounds around you. Listen well. Now choose just one of the sounds — a bird's twitter, or a distant buzzing, a faint clicking, or a persistent roar. Whatever it is, go into the sound. Really listen to it, riding on the waves of the sound.

- Now turn your attention to your sense of touch. Let your hand reach for an object that is lying nearby. A book, perhaps, or a vase, or a twig, or a blade of grass. Touch it with full awareness. Feel its texture. Feel whether it is hard or soft, cold or warm. Let your sense of touch come alive to this object. Let your fingers linger there for some moments.

- Now sharpen your sense of smell. Bring your attention to the aromas in the air. At first you may simply be smelling fresh or stale air. Continue to focus on your sense of smell and allow yourself to pick up the details of what you can smell. Don't worry if you can't discern particular smells; what counts is that you are taking the time to focus on this particular sense.

Finish this exercise by sitting quietly for a few moments, taking care to breathe regularly. Then ease yourself into whatever you need to do next.

You'll notice that the sense of taste is not included here. Try this separately, at your next mealtime perhaps. Eat slowly and deliberately, concentrating on each mouthful and noticing the taste of your food.

Finding your intuitive state

An intuitive state is simply one of waiting and openness. It is not a mystical state of being, or a state available to very few. You yourself have been in an intuitive state, but you might not have described your experience that way.

Most of the time, your conscious mind is active, working on facts, using logic, moving sequentially. What being in an intuitive state requires is that you detach from that for the time being. With your mind buzzing wildly, intuition is unlikely to make itself known. You may indeed have a flash of insight, an experience of intuition, when you are busy and involved, but it's more likely to happen when you've allowed yourself practice in quietening the mind.

There are a number of ways that you can encourage an intuitive frame of mind:

- Go walking, or running, or swimming. Just get your body moving so that the mind is not in control, chattering at you about *shoulds* and schedules and deadlines.
- Breathe deeply. Stand or sit comfortably and feel your body come to life with each breath. Feel the stale energy leave your body as you exhale.
- Take up yoga or t'ai chi. Apart from keeping you supple, relaxed and toned physically, such practices encourage a still, focused mind.
- Listen to music. 'Life seems to go on without effort when I have music,' said the writer George Eliot. You'll reach an intuitive state without effort if you listen to music.
- Meditate or pray. These practices will induce a more receptive state of being; that is, you will be more open to receiving intuitive information.
- Spend time in an environment that is restful. You might choose to be by the water, or among trees, or spend time indoors, where your surroundings give you deep pleasure. Simply be where you can relax totally.
- Give yourself over to daydreaming. When you daydream, impossible things seem possible, and your intuition has a chance to play with such possibilities.

Exercise — Learning about your intuitive state

This exercise will help you identify your own intuitive state by locating some of the details in your body. This will allow you both to recognise when you are being intuitive, and to enter into that state more easily on a regular basis.

- Make yourself comfortable, relax, close your eyes, and focus on your breath. In … out … in … out …
- Start to imagine yourself thinking intuitively … Take some time to imagine this state, and then ask yourself these questions:
  » How do I know when I am thinking intuitively?
  » What do I look like?
  » What do I sound like?
  » How do I feel?
  » What physical sensations do I notice in my body?

Using fantasy, imagination and dreams

Imagination is more important than knowledge. Knowledge is limited. Imagination encircles the world.
ALBERT EINSTEIN, PHYSICIST

Imagine this: a mind so used to reasoning and analysing, applying logic and striving for solutions as soon as possible that it no longer remembers how to play. No flights of fancy. No wild imaginings. No free play.

If it sounds to you like a prison, then you've recognised the fantastic freedom that is available in fantasy, in imagination, and in dreams. To put all your energy into mind work – the rational, logical, analytical sort, is to straitjacket yourself, to choke off the sustenance that the life of the imagination offers you.

Imagination and fantasy counterbalance logic and reason.

One of the most alarming aspects of some children's lives these days is that they are allowed little time for play. Living in a world of adult structure and involved constantly in adult-directed activities, they have no opportunity to engage in playful games, to exercise their imaginations, to play 'what if'. Given this, they are at risk of losing the intuitive abilities nourished by childhood fantasy.

When you use your imagination, when you embark on flights of fantasy, you are:

- Surrendering to greater possibilities;
- Breathing new life into the everyday;
- Inviting a greater force to join you in play;
- Breaking through the boundaries of limiting belief systems that keep you bound to 'reality';
- Nourishing your intuitive powers.

> *We have forgotten the fact that God speaks chiefly through dreams and visions.*
> CARL JUNG, PSYCHOLOGIST AND PSYCHIATRIST

Dreams

Dreams can reveal much about your life that, during waking hours, is difficult to recognise. During sleep, subconscious processes are at work, making connections, sorting, making some sort of sense out of your everyday experience (however mysterious this may seem on waking).

The images in dreams can be confounding. However, over time you may start to see patterns and identify images that appear regularly. This, in turn, will help your intuitive powers, because the images in dreams and in flashes of intuition are personal to you.

Here is how you can make your dreams work for you:

1. Tell yourself before you go to sleep that you will remember tonight's dreams.
2. Keep a pen and paper (or a journal) by your bed.
3. On waking, keep your eyes closed and stay still.
4. Grab a fragment of the dream and hold onto it. Let it lead you to the next bit ...
5. Let the dream lie loosely until you feel you have most, or all, of it.
6. Write the dream down, recording the date.
7. Be patient in deciphering the dream. It may be immediately obvious, but don't jump to conclusions.
8. Read over your dreams from time to time – they may make more sense later.
9. Don't work too hard at understanding a dream – if your subconscious wants to give you a message, it will try again, perhaps in another way.

Images and symbols

Dreams appear in images, and classical dream theory says that they reveal the inner depths of the individual. Your longings and fears are expressed in terms of familiar images, although the meaning of any particular dream is rarely immediately obvious. It takes some time and conscious thought to unravel its mysteries.

Central to understanding dreams is the deciphering of symbols. In other words, what do certain images represent? What do they symbolise? They can mean different things to different people. Here is an example of how images and symbols can differ in meaning from one person to another:

A dream of someone alone in a little boat, at night in the dark, may be unsettling for one person. It may conjure up a feeling of danger, of extreme vulnerability, of impending doom. A boat may be a symbol for them of aloneness and abandonment, of being left to cope with the 'sea of life' on one's own. For another person, such a dream may be a comfortable and comforting one, invoking the extreme pleasure that can come from solitude. The dark, the quiet, the stillness, may all represent a respite from the busy-ness and madness of daily living.

Just as many of the images and symbols that appear in your dreams are unique to you in terms of the meaning, so much of the imagery and symbolism in your intuitions is also unique to you. Not everyone experiences their intuition through imagery, but if you do, building a 'dictionary' of intuitive vocabulary as a guide to interpreting your intuitions can be helpful.

Use the following exercise to get you started, and if you find it difficult to record information from your intuitive experiences, then use your dreams as a guide. Do it in the morning, while your dreams are fresh, and simply jot down what appeared in your dreams and your responses. Then, little by little, do the same with your intuitive experiences.

You might like to keep a special book for your dictionary. Or you could incorporate it into your intuitive journal, perhaps keeping the dictionary part at the back, where it's easy to find each time you want to refer to it or add to it.

A word of warning: the danger in this approach can be over-analysis and a rigid 'definition' of the meaning of the imagery you find recurring in your intuitions. You can avoid this danger by staying open to the possibilities that the imagery presents, and by remembering that coming to hard and fast conclusions runs contrary to the place of intuition in your life.

Exercise — Compile your own dictionary of intuitive vocabulary

This is an exercise that will help you become familiar with your own intuitive vocabulary. Complete the following statements and record your responses in your dictionary.

- When I am happy, I feel …
- A positive visual image for me is …
- A negative visual image for me is …
- When I think of the colour red, I think of …; with blue, I think of …; with yellow, I think of …; with black, I think of … etc.
- For me, the image of the sun means …
- For me, the image of the moon means …
- When a person says 'no' to me, I feel …

Continue in this way, answering questions as they arise, and so compile your own personal dictionary of intuitive symbolism.

Nurturing your intuition

What does one feed intuition so that it is consistently nourished and responsive to our requests to scan our environs? One feeds it life – one feeds it life by listening to it. What good is a voice without an ear to receive it?
CLARISSA PINKOLA ESTÉS, JUNGIAN ANALYST AND AUTHOR

Once you have awakened your intuition, you won't want to starve it of attention, or allow it to diminish because you don't know what you could be doing to keep it alive and well. Here are some ways to continue nurturing your intuitive powers. You may find it useful to note down these nurturing approaches in your journal, adding to them as you expand your own personal approach, and adding other ways as they occur to you.

- **Live in the moment.** Most people have great difficulty with this, rushing as they do from one activity to another, or caught up in multiple responsibilities. But while you have your senses focused on anything but the present, you are likely to miss out on intuitive possibilities. Practise bringing your full attention to every activity, every moment, in your day.
- **Remain observant.** Sometimes intuitive moments are passed over because they appear in ways you never expected. Some of you may feel your hunches in the body – a twinge, an itch, a chill, for example. Others may experience strong intuitive messages through dreams or other visual images; others again may hear words or sounds that trigger intuition. By keeping a record of your experiences, you may notice patterns emerging, and you will become more attuned to those signals of intuition that might otherwise have gone unnoticed.

- **Practise your intuitive powers.** Try it now: think of something you would like an answer to, and allow any answer to float into your consciousness. Make a note of it, and possibly act on it, but don't question where it came from. Just let it be. Start practising in a variety of situations: for example, as you leave home in the morning take a few seconds to imagine who you might bump into today, or what events might happen. Whether you get it right or not is not the point. All you are doing is experiencing the receiving of information rather than doing the usual mental exercise that a purely rational approach entails.
- **Learn to be more receptive.** This means moving into a state where you are able to hear the quiet voice of intuition, however it expresses itself. There are a few ways you could improve your receptivity. Some people like to use a creative visualisation that involves meeting up with an inner guide or teacher. Some people find prayer a wonderful way to open up. Meditation will also bring you to a more receptive state of being, where intuitive thoughts are more likely to appear. See the exercise *Listen deeply*, a form of meditation, on the following page.
- **Relax, especially after times of using logic and reason.** Many people report times of great insight after their intellect has been used intensively and then rested. It is as though the subconscious swings into action providing what would never surface during intense rational moments. It can be no coincidence that many intellectual discoveries have been made in the bath, or during a quiet walk, or sitting on a bus.
- **Trust yourself.** As you practise your intuition, as you identify and acknowledge it, you will grow more confident in your ability to recognise it and act on it. This may take time, especially if you are a person who has until now relied largely on logic and analysis in making decisions. This may be a new approach for you, but it is just as valid. In time, you will discover that integrating your intuitive powers with the powers of your intellect is exciting, satisfying and enriching.

Exercise — Listen deeply

- Start by doing the exercise *Relax your ever-active mind* (page 41).

- Continue to sit quietly, and listen for silence. This exercise may take some time, because you may be used to listening for noise. Be patient. Keep sitting with yourself.

- It may be a while before you experience it, but there will be a moment when you touch a profound sense of quiet. You may feel that it is deep within you. Keep sitting, even if the moment is fleeting.

- Allow some curiosity to surface. 'What is this quiet place?' Wait. Listen.

- You'll find that after sitting in this way, thoughts and images will start to emerge. Notice them. Acknowledge them. They are worth attention because they have surfaced from the still place within you.

Harnessing your intuition

Knowing what you want

> *What's terrible is to pretend that the second-rate is first-rate. To pretend that you don't need love when you do; or you like your work when you know quite well you're capable of better.*
> DORIS LESSING, AUTHOR

So many people, the author Henry David Thoreau said, lead lives of 'quiet desperation'. He was talking about the ordinary person in the Western world, a person who is clothed and fed and sheltered. What is there to be desperate about?

Could it be that they don't know what they really want? Is it that they are pretending to live first-rate lives when, in fact, they are settling for far less? Are you one of these people?

Some people protest that they don't think about what they really want because they can't have it anyway. And if what they really want is, for example, to retire tonight with millions of dollars in the bank, houses all around the world, and several private jets to get them there, then they may be right. But is this what you would really want?

It's worth giving this question some serious thought, because what emerges might surprise you. Here is an example: Jerry believes that what he really wants is lots of money. Sometimes he falls into despair because the amount he's decided he'd like to have is out of his reach, given the work he does. This is a theme of his life: wishing for much more money, and then long periods of despair and frustration.

However, question Jerry further and this is what you might hear: that if he had money, he would feel better about himself, and this would mean he would enjoy his work more, and this would improve his relationships with his wife and children, and so his life would be wonderful. If only he had more money.

If Jerry could stand back from this, he would see that what he wants is to enjoy his work and to have good relationships with his wife and children. By deciding that it is money that will make the difference, he keeps short-circuiting his own path to satisfaction.

In other words, Jerry is jumping to what he thinks is the solution to his 'problem' rather than reflecting deeply on what he wants in life. By concentrating on what he thinks is the answer, he is cutting off other possibilities of getting what he would really like. And he is short-circuiting messages from his intuition, which may be giving him clues about how to move forwards. Sad, isn't it? But Jerry's story is a common one.

You may find that you aren't sure of what you want, but you do know what you don't want. Whether you do know what you want or you don't, the following exercises will be helpful in pinpointing your deepest desires.

The importance of knowing what you want is that it clears the way for greater intuitive awareness. Lack of clarity about direction and desire will mask subtle messages from your intuition. When you know what it is you want, you can visualise it and then ask for it. And your intuition will answer every time.

Exercise — What do I want?

Use your journal for this exercise, which begins with a personal brainstorming session:

- Get comfortable and focus on your breathing for a few moments.

- Now jot down whatever arises when you ask yourself: 'What do I really want?'

- Remember that this section of the exercise is a brainstorming session, so don't judge your responses. For example, if 'money' comes to mind or 'a dishwasher', don't dismiss them as being superficial or inappropriate wants. Jot them down, along with everything else that comes to you.

- Keep asking yourself gently: 'What do I really want?' And keep on jotting down what comes into your mind. Write your responses all over the page and in different colours – this helps the spontaneous, intuitive responses.

- When you feel that you have come to a natural end, sit quietly and read over what you've written down. You might like to circle some responses and make links on the page. Don't force this part of the exercise. Allow it to happen naturally.

- As you reflect on these responses, what you really want will become clearer to you. Be prepared for sudden insights, for wonderful surprises.

Some exercises follow in this book to help you move forwards from this point. You will find it useful to return to the exercise *What do I want?* every so often, perhaps when you are feeling restless or confused and seeking clarity.

You may discover that as your circumstances change, so too does what you really want. Do the exercise every two months, both to check on your heart's desire and also to remind yourself of it.

Using creative visualisation

Developing and harnessing your intuition will allow you to access answers to any question you might have about your life. This doesn't mean that you will overcome all life's challenges and struggles easily and quickly. What it does mean is that you will feel clearer about the way ahead. You will not be lost in the confusion and chaos of uncertainty and insecurity.

In the next section, you will learn about how to pose the questions. But before you begin asking those questions, there is a powerful exercise that will help you formulate them. As you will see, this exercise also has other benefits. It is the process of creative visualisation.

Creative visualisation is the art of imagination, involving the conjuring up of visual imagery. If your response to this is that you can't imagine visually, then try this quick exercise: think of a friend you haven't seen for a while, and see their face smiling at you.

The image may not be distinct, but you'll find that there will be an 'essence' of the person's features that appears in your mind. Try another little exercise: close your eyes and think of a blue sky with soft powdery clouds drifting by. See the picture in your mind's eye. These little exercises will give you a 'flavour' of what visualising entails.

Creative visualisation has been used in many contexts. It is used by patients to imagine their bodies strong and well, for example. It is used by sportspeople to imagine themselves playing their games the best they possibly can. It is used by people every day to imagine themselves interacting with others and completing their work in a way that is considerate and satisfying. Starting your day in this way can be very rewarding.

To help you formulate questions for your intuition, start with this simple exercise. Record your responses in your journal.

Exercise — I am happy and content

- Sit comfortably and close your eyes. Focus on your breathing; breathe gently and slowly and rhythmically.
- Now see yourself in your mind's eye. Imagine that you are deeply happy and content, and your days are filled with light. Imagine yourself in this state. How do you look? How do you feel?
- Go on imagining that you are happy and content. How do you interact with those closest to you? What do you do? How do you feel? How do you relate to others you meet? What do you do? How do you feel?
- Imagine yourself at work. You are deeply happy and content. What is happening? How do you go about what you do?
- Focus on your breathing once again, and slowly come back to where you are sitting.

The beauty of this exercise is that it allows you to imagine what you yearn for. Living out your ideal self and ideal life in this virtual way through creatively visualising them helps you identify what holds you back, and opens you to all manner of intuitive possibilities.

On the next page is another creative visualisation exercise that allows you to imagine a safe place for yourself, a place you can retreat to when you need space in your life, and when you want to be still in a surrounding of your choice. Going there can free you from the constraints you experience in your everyday life, and offer you a place where you can receive intuitive information.

Exercise — A safe place for inspiration

To gain the most from this exercise, try asking someone to read the words below quietly and slowly to you, or tape yourself speaking them and play it back. Start by getting yourself into a comfortable position, in as quiet a spot as possible.

- Now that you are comfortable, focus on your breath ... imagine yourself breathing in relaxation and breathing out tension ... relaxation in ... tension out ...

- Now feel your body becoming lighter and lighter ... you begin to rise into the air and you are floating free ... you feel lighter and freer than ever before ... up, up, up towards the cloudless sky you float ... you feel light, airless, carefree ... there is nothing to weigh you down ... you keep floating on ... breathing in relaxation ... you are light ... lighter than a feather ...

- Decide on a quiet, safe spot for you to be ... it may be a cave or a valley, by the water or on a hilltop ... begin to circle down to this favourite place ... land softly in this favourite place ... settle comfortably and look around you ... everything here gives you pleasure ...

- Settle yourself safely and rest quietly ... there are no time restrictions here ... just simply be ... feel yourself just being here ... safe ... quiet ...

- Be open to any message that might come ... it may be in the form of an image, or a sound, or a taste ... be open to whatever comes ...

- When you feel ready, begin to focus back on your breathing ... take a few breaths to energise yourself ... become aware of where you are now, of where you are sitting ... be confident that you are refreshed and energised and that you are ready to face whatever is next ... your life is unfolding as it should and all is well ...

Asking the right questions

Ask, and it shall be given you.
MATTHEW 7:6

The exercise *What do I want?* (page 59) and the visualisation *I am happy and content* (page 61) will help you identify what is most important to you. This step is essential if you are to be clear about the way forward for you. Otherwise, you may find yourself waiting for intuitive responses to questions such as:

- How can I be happier?
- How can I improve my relationships?
- Which is the best job for me out of these possibilities?

These questions are perfectly fine, up to a point. They are questions people ask themselves every day, as they search for contentment and fulfilment in life. But they are vague and non-specific questions, and any intuitive responses may be lost in the 'bigness' of each question.

For example, take the first question: 'How can I be happier?' It leads immediately into these other, more detailed questions:

- Happier than what?
- Happier than whom?
- What does happy mean for me?
- How much happiness is enough?
- Do I mean just a tiny bit happier, or a lot, lot happier?

As Jody's story (following) indicates, one question can mask many, many questions that need to be addressed. This is part of the clarifying process. Practise your questions. Think of a question now, something that you would like an answer to in your life, and write it in your journal. Notice your wording. Is it specific? Is it simple? Is it unambiguous?

Personal Story
Unpacking the question

Jody has been committed to developing her intuitive powers for some years now. She says that they have grown as she has come to trust them more, and she spends some time meditating each day, and reflecting on what she wants to ask. 'The nature of the question is very important,' she says.

'I found this out a couple of years ago, when I decided I wanted an answer to this question: 'Should I take this job that's been offered to me?' I suppose I expected a 'no' or a 'yes.' It seemed easy enough. But when I had no sense of an answer and time was marching on, I sat down with the question and unpacked it. I realised that there were a lot more questions involved in there, many sub-questions that needed to be addressed first. I had to do some unpacking.

'What sort of work did I really want anyway? What did I find most satisfying? What salary was I happy with? What amount of time did I want free to spend with my family? These questions may not apply to everybody, but they certainly did to me. So, I brainstormed all the questions that occurred to me, and spent some time on each of them before I made the final decision.'

The art of interpretation

While intuition may appear as a thought, it does not present as a logical sequence of ideas or a list of 'things to do'. It is more likely to appear as a metaphor or a symbol or an image. And just as you need to interpret your dreams, so you need to interpret what arrives through intuition. The data may appear as you are engaged in some completely unrelated activity. It might be a sense that makes itself known in your body and then emerges as a more specific piece of information. It may come as an image, a symbol or a picture.

After the receiving of the data comes the translation, or interpretation. This can be tricky. A common mistake is to rush to interpret it, but haste is no friend of intuition. The imagery that comes through intuition can be very puzzling, and the unravelling can take some time. Of course, you may understand immediately, you may have a flash of great insight, but even then, if you remain receptive to the message, you'll find that more will be revealed over time. You may have an 'aha!' experience very quickly, and that may be followed by a further 'aha!' days or weeks later, when you've had a chance to process the intuitive message.

Many times, though, you have to let the message rest lightly in your consciousness, incubating slowly and surely. Revisit it every so often, look at it from different angles, and let it go again to do its own work at its own pace. In the meantime, write down any insights in your journal, and refer to your personal dictionary, adding to it when appropriate. With patience and openness and intent, you will find the wisdom of your intuition will reveal itself one way or another.

In interpreting your intuitive messages, be wary of wishful thinking and fear. Wishful thinking can lead you to read into your intuition all sorts of wants and desires. For example: 'My intuition tells me I am meant to have that person as my partner.' Some honest self-examination will reveal to you whether or not you are simply using intuition to justify your wish for a certain outcome.

Fear can also be projected onto intuitive messages. For example, if you say that 'My intuition tells me I should not try for a different job', it may in fact be the voice of fear and self-doubt, not intuition, holding you back.

Personal Story
Interpreting drifts

Casey is a fabric designer. She tells the story of a particular client who asked her to come up with a design for the fabric in her new studio. 'Each time I talked to this client, the song 'Moon River' would come into my mind. I have no idea why,' Casey says.

'When I started on the design, I took the song seriously. I felt sure it was intuitive symbolism, and I wanted to follow my intuition. The client had given me free rein, so I used moon motifs in soft gold against a soft, watery blue wash.

'The client loved it. When she saw it, the first thing she said was 'Moon River'! I've always thought of myself as a bit of a "Holly Golightly"! Maybe I picked up on that during our conversations. Certainly nothing was spoken about it. What I do know is that I felt the importance of interpreting the drifts of song that kept playing over and over in my head.'

Intuition and reason together

Your intuitive faculty is immensely valuable. However, to decide that you will use it to the exclusion of your faculty for reason and logic would be as limiting as if you relied only on your intellect to guide you. It is only by working with intuition and reason together that you work with your 'whole brain'.

In fact, you are using the two together whether or not you are aware of it. By expressing your intuitive messages in language, and by interpreting them to make sense to you, you are employing your 'left brain' to translate a 'right brain' experience.

The following exercise, *Intuition and reason working together*, will take you inside yourself to greet your intellect and your intuition. It is a way to befriend these parts of yourself, and to encourage them to work together.

Exercise — Intuition and reason working together

- Make yourself comfortable. Close your eyes and focus on your breath for a few moments.

- Imagine yourself going 'inside', to where your intellect and your intuition lie.

- Go up to each one of them and take a good look. Pick each one up if you like, hold it this way and that.

- How does your intellect look? Does it reason well? Does it use logic well? Is it tight or loose? Is it heavy or light? Look at it carefully. Thank it for serving you well.

- How does your intuition look? Is it vibrant and alive? Is it quiet and retiring? Look at it closely. Thank it for serving you well.

- When you leave this place, thank both your intellect and your intuition for working together so well, and encourage them to work together even better.

- Focus on your breath again, and after a few moments, open your eyes.

Is it really intuition?

How do we know when the message we feel we are receiving is truly intuition and not something else? Here are some clues that will reveal the difference to you:

- Test the 'intuition' by considering whether it is charged with either positive or negative emotion. True intuition is neutral, matter-of-fact thought; you may feel anxious or nervous or excited afterwards, but not at the time of the intuitive 'thought'.
- Know yourself. Certain feelings will distort intuition, and if you know how you would normally react in certain situations, you can take that into account when you have some sense of intuition. For example, if you are leaving on a trip and begin to feel anxious and wary, consider how you normally feel in this situation before taking note of what seem to be intuitive feelings.
- Keep a record of your intuitive experiences. Note down the thought (or symbol, or image), the date, what you were doing at the time, how it felt, whether or not you acted on the intuition, and what finally happened. This way, over time you can learn to recognise moments of true intuition.

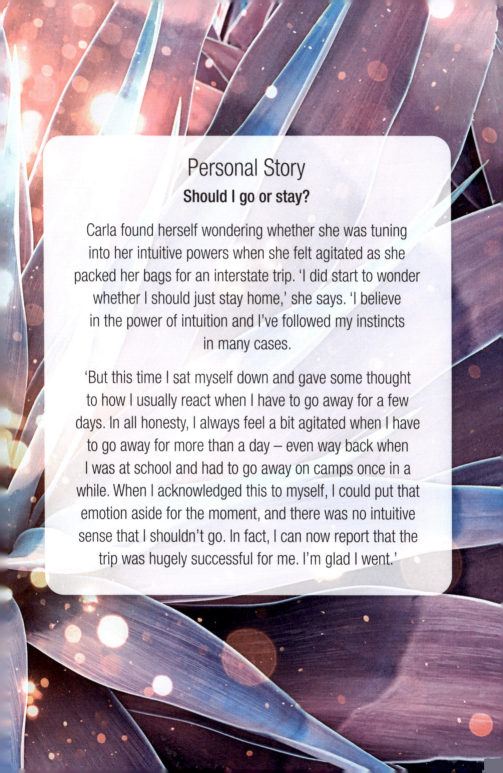

Personal Story
Should I go or stay?

Carla found herself wondering whether she was tuning into her intuitive powers when she felt agitated as she packed her bags for an interstate trip. 'I did start to wonder whether I should just stay home,' she says. 'I believe in the power of intuition and I've followed my instincts in many cases.

'But this time I sat myself down and gave some thought to how I usually react when I have to go away for a few days. In all honesty, I always feel a bit agitated when I have to go away for more than a day — even way back when I was at school and had to go away on camps once in a while. When I acknowledged this to myself, I could put that emotion aside for the moment, and there was no intuitive sense that I shouldn't go. In fact, I can now report that the trip was hugely successful for me. I'm glad I went.'

Intuition in action

Everyday intuition

Your intuition does not need to be saved for special occasions. It is something that can be called on day by day, minute by minute. If you put the processes in this book into practice, you will not only awaken your intuition, but also develop it and harness it in a way that benefits you in every area of your life. At first, you may be self-conscious about using your intuition, but over time it will become second nature to you. You will call on your intuition as easily as you draw breath.

Over the page are some ways to start practising your everyday intuition. Some of the ideas may seem flippant, but remember, your intuition can be fun-loving, just as your faculties for imagining and daydreaming are. You will think of your own ways to apply your intuition – record them in your journal and practise them often.

Keep in mind, too, that the point is not to 'get it right' every time. This is no test or exam, with marks to indicate your degree of success. What counts here is that you have a go. You aren't a failure if you get it 'wrong'. You are simply playing, and your intuition will gradually strengthen and expand and deepen as you exercise it.

> It is in the highest degree astonishing to see what a large number of general theorems, the methodical deduction of which requires the highest powers of mathematical analysis, he found by a kind of intuition, with the security of instinct, without the help of a single mathematical formula.

Hermann Von Helmholtz, physicist,
speaking of Michael Faraday, physical scientist

Everyday games for your intuition

- For the next week, give yourself just a few seconds to decide what to wear for the day. Let your intuition guide you as to what is appropriate.
- Next time the phone rings, in fact, every time it rings, guess who is calling before answering.
- When you've been occupied for a while, guess what time you think it is before checking your watch.
- Shuffle a pack of cards, and pick a card out, face down. Take a guess at the suit (or the specific card) before turning it over.
- Before checking what's in the mail, guess what's there.

And for more fun, try this exercise. Use your journal to jot down an answer for each of the following. Give yourself only three seconds to respond to each one:

- A girl's name;
- A boy's name;
- A type of animal;
- A red object;
- The name of a book;
- Something soft;
- The name of a river.

These are simply triggers for your intuition. Notice over the next week or two how what you wrote down as your responses appears in your life in various ways: in conversation, in reading, in the media. This last exercise will strengthen your powers of attention and observation.

Developing problem-solving techniques

Whenever you are faced with a problem, it is only natural to wish for a quick, easy solution. Unfortunately, many problems can't be dealt with quickly and easily. There are circumstances you have to learn to live with, situations you have to come to terms with.

At the same time, you can find yourself weighed down with a problem when that burden could be eased. Certainly, many people attest to the value of meditation or prayer at such times.

There are times, too, when it is appropriate to sharpen your problem-solving techniques. The ups and downs of life can leave you weary, and it's easy to forget that you have the ability to solve many problems using your intuitive powers.

Processes already presented in this book will help with your problem-solving. Below is another process to use when you are faced with a dilemma. Have your journal and pen ready.

Process: wanting to solve a problem

- Find a comfortable position, and close your eyes. Focus on your breathing for a few moments.
- See in your mind's eye the problem you want to solve. See it in front of you in as much detail as possible. If you find it difficult to conjure up images, then pretend that you can see the problem there.
- Say: 'I want direction here. How can I see this differently?'
- Walk around the problem, looking at it from different angles. How does it look? How does it feel? How does it sound?
- As you sit with this problem in your mind's eye, feel sure that all will be resolved. Say to yourself: 'All is well. I trust that all will be resolved.'
- Focus on your breathing for a few moments, then open your eyes. Jot down in your journal any thoughts, symbols, insights that you have had.
- Allow your intuitive powers to do their work as you move on to other things.

Intuition on the job

Are you bored with life? Then throw yourself into some work you believe in with all your heart, live for it, die for it, and you find happiness that you had thought could never be yours.
DALE CARNEGIE, AUTHOR AND MOTIVATOR

Finding 'the perfect job' can be a consuming activity for some people. When you feel restless, unappreciated, overworked or bored, your job can become an easy target for your frustration. 'If I were working in the right job, I wouldn't feel this way. I'd be happy/content/fulfilled.'

Occasional frustration with your work is nothing to be concerned about. However, if you frequently feel unhappy and dissatisfied, it might be time to take action.

- Take some time and work through the exercise *What do I want?* (page 59). Hand over to your intuition the work of telling you what's most important to you. Be alert to images, symbols, ideas, insights.
- Be prepared to act on your intuition, whatever its message.
- Practise self-awareness and self-examination so that you can more easily discern the meaning of any intuitive messages.
- Accept that you may be guided to leave your present employment, and that you will not be left stranded.
- Say to yourself: 'I am wanting direction here. I am wanting to move past my fear. I am open to guidance.'

Personal Story
Using intuition for guidance

Bryan is a sales manager for a large sporting equipment company. He uses his intuition, he says, when interviewing people with a view to hiring them. 'I go by my gut feeling about people,' he says. 'You might be surprised at some of the people I've said no to. They look good, sound great, they have all it takes on paper, but there's something missing. Or else there's something there that just isn't right.

'Some of the people I've hired haven't had that glossy look or impeccable records. But I was prepared to take them on – they felt right to me. I can't think of an instance when I've regretted it. I think when you're employing people, you have to rely on that sixth sense because you can't always trust what you see on the surface.'

Using intuition at work

As in other areas of your life, you use your intuition often in your workplace, whether or not you realise it. You use it when you:

- Prioritise your work commitments;
- Disclose or withhold information;
- Approach a colleague who seems to need support.

These are all instances of intuition at work. Take some time now to record in your journal instances of using your intuition at work over the past week. Reflect on how using your intuition more would change the way you work, then jot down in your journal five additional ways you could use your intuition in the workplace.

Intuition in business

> *The ability to blend the seemingly diverse worlds of business and intuition can precipitate a well-managed and efficient organisation whose bottom-line profits could only be matched by the joy, success and fulfilment its employees and owners receive.*
> JOHN HARRICHARAN, AUTHOR AND LECTURER

Increasingly, businesses are turning to experts in the field of intuition for help in learning how to access this powerful tool. Whether it is to shape decisions, assess business relationships, or decide on a course of action, business leaders are recognising that intuition can guide them.

By respecting the roles of logic and reason and intuition, and acknowledging the importance of working with all of them together, business leaders are honouring the 'whole-brain' concept. The results? Greater innovation, creative and workable strategies, motivated employees, and increased profits all round.

Personal Story
Please apply!

Five years ago, Deidre knew she had to do something about her life. 'I needed to change direction,' she says. 'Things weren't working for me. I was in a financial trough, and I had to do something about that. I spent some time settling myself, listening to my intuition, and felt strongly that I needed to go back to teaching. I'd left it for a while to pursue other work.

'Now I felt sure this was the right path for me, and the following Saturday I saw a position advertised that sounded perfect. In fact, it may as well have said "Deidre, please apply. We have the perfect job for you." I went for an interview, and from the first minute I knew this was "my job". Doubt never entered my mind. I went home and started preparing for the position, well before I finally heard that it was mine. I'd never been more sure of anything in my life.'

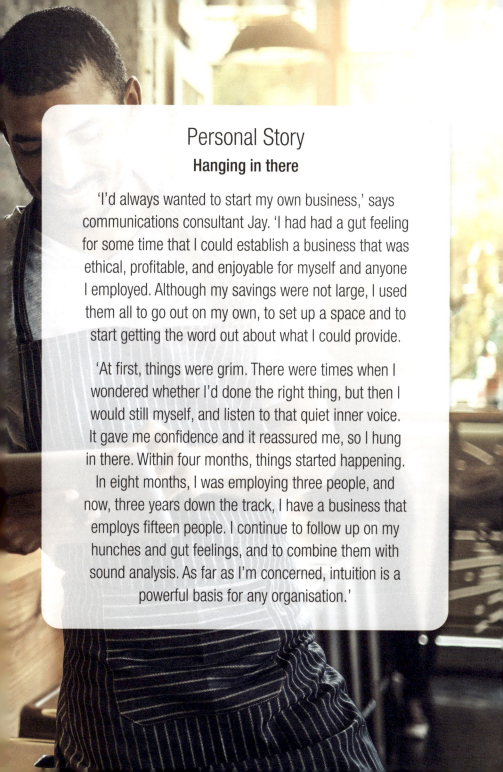

Personal Story
Hanging in there

'I'd always wanted to start my own business,' says communications consultant Jay. 'I had had a gut feeling for some time that I could establish a business that was ethical, profitable, and enjoyable for myself and anyone I employed. Although my savings were not large, I used them all to go out on my own, to set up a space and to start getting the word out about what I could provide.

'At first, things were grim. There were times when I wondered whether I'd done the right thing, but then I would still myself, and listen to that quiet inner voice. It gave me confidence and it reassured me, so I hung in there. Within four months, things started happening. In eight months, I was employing three people, and now, three years down the track, I have a business that employs fifteen people. I continue to follow up on my hunches and gut feelings, and to combine them with sound analysis. As far as I'm concerned, intuition is a powerful basis for any organisation.'

Intuition, medicine and healing

Alphabetic methods have to be replaced with more intuitive methods. Intuition is behind every diagnosis, formulation, patient contact. If it weren't, I'd be an analytic machine.
DR OLIVER SACKS, NEUROLOGIST AND AUTHOR

It would be reassuring to believe that medical diagnoses are easy to make, and that health practitioners use the wonders of science to uncover both the nature and the cause of all illnesses. But every one of us has stories of diagnoses that were wrong, and of treatments that caused more problems than the illness itself. The truth is, health practitioners are not infallible, nor are their methods.

Scientific breakthroughs are good news, but so too is the fact that many health practitioners are relying on their intuition to help them help their patients – and saying so. Reliance on established procedures alone is making way for an increasing respect for the role of intuition in diagnoses. Like Dr Sacks, many doctors and other specialists are using 'more intuitive methods', trusting hunches to help guide them in their diagnoses and treatments.

Personal Story
It's a miracle!

Joe is a doctor who has augmented his orthodox qualifications with study in herbal medicine and acupuncture. 'From my point of view,' he says, 'it would be unusual for a doctor or other practitioner to never use intuition. In fact, I'd say it must be impossible.

'As a doctor, you hear about the patient's symptoms, and sometimes they are detailed and it is easy to make a diagnosis. But very often it isn't as clear as all that. You have to use a sixth sense, a gut instinct, your intuition. You follow up on those hunches, of course. But we aren't machines, we can't always know for sure.

'I can remember one patient in particular, an elderly man who was ill but couldn't quite articulate what was going on. I sat quietly with him for a while, and then I asked a couple of questions that were based on hunches of mine. He was amazed, and acted as though it was a miracle that I'd been able to uncover the problem. But it was no miracle – unless you like to call ordinary old intuitive powers miraculous!'

The practice of intuition

Using objects to guide you

Although intuition lies within you, you can use objects to help you access your intuitive messages. This is a helpful exercise when you have a particular question you would like answered, or a problem for which you want guidance.

Use your journal to record your impressions and insights.

1. Reflect for a few minutes on the question or the situation about which you want more information. Write it down, clarifying it as you write.
2. Sit comfortably and quietly, allowing the question to rest with you.
3. Start walking slowly around the room, or even further, picking up as you go three objects that catch your eye. At this stage, give no thought to your choice. Simply pick up three objects your eyes are drawn to.
4. Now lay the objects out in front of you, in order of significance. Tune in to your intuitive powers to guide you as to the order of significance.
5. For a few moments, focus on your breathing. Sit quietly and feel the wisdom within you. Feel the wisdom glowing brightly there.
6. Take up the first object you chose, and reflect on it. What is it? How is it used? What is its history for you? Ask yourself what symbolism lies here. How is this object linked to your question? How is it symbolically related?
7. Write down all your impressions, everything that emerges as you reflect on this first object.
8. Turn to the second object. As you reflect on the object, ask yourself 'What is holding me back here?' Spend some time regarding the object, noticing the symbolism, and jotting down in your journal all that emerges.
9. Now turn to the third object, looking at it carefully. Ask yourself 'What is the appropriate step to take here?' Again, what is this object symbolising for you? Write down all that comes to you as you continue to reflect on it.
10. Look over what you have written down, and use the following *Personal story* as a guide in deciphering what you've written down.

Personal Story
Following the inner voice

When Sarah did this exercise, her question was: 'Should I leave this relationship I'm in?' She picked up a red vase, a photo of her family and a small lamp. This is how the objects were guided by her intuition.

'The red vase is a favourite of mine, given to me by my sister years ago. I realised that I hadn't filled it with beautiful flowers for a long time, and that was a sign to me of how diminished I was feeling these days. There was something here too of not feeding my passion.

'The photo of my family guided me with the question of what is holding me back. I felt concerned that they would judge me, that they would criticise me if I left this relationship, even if it is not a good one for me. In the past, this has been difficult, and I sensed my reluctance to be exposed to that criticism again.

'The lamp said right away to me "Bring some light into your life." I had a sense of darkness when I reflected on this object, as though I'd been there too long now.

'This exercise helped me with my decision – I see so clearly now what I have to do. If I do what I feel is right for me, my family will understand, even if it takes time. I have to follow my inner voice, not be paralysed by what people might think of me.'

Your intuitive style

By now, you are aware that intuition makes itself known in images, in flashes, in symbolism, in fragments. It is very rare to be presented with a complete picture, a literal unfolding of events or circumstances.

Consider this example: Irene was on holiday in a remote area, and during the second week of her trip, she felt a strong urge to phone her mother. She says it was like a nagging voice, and she had a sense of being physically tugged. She responded to this intuitive call and contacted her mother, to learn that her father had been admitted to hospital just a few hours before with a suspected heart attack. Her mother was relieved to hear from her, and Irene made a quick change of plans so that she could be with her dearly loved dad. Note that in this story, Irene did not 'receive' a clear, detailed picture of what had happened. But her intuition, in the form of a 'nagging voice' and 'a physical tug', did alert her.

Most experiences of intuition are not warnings of such dramatic circumstances. Our everyday intuition can guide us in the simplest of decisions. You might use it, for example, to find your way to somewhere you've never visited before. You might exercise it in deciding what to wear for the day. You may call on your intuition to help you prioritise the day's work. However you use your intuition, and in whatever ways you would like to strengthen it, it is helpful to understand your own individual intuitive style. On the next page is an exercise to get you started.

Exercise — Where is your intuition?

- Sit comfortably, and focus on your breathing for a few moments.
- Tune in to the intuitive part of you and reflect on your intuition. Imagine yourself in an intuitive state. You may find it helpful to imagine a time when you had a hunch or a gut instinct about something.
- As you reflect on this intuitive state, ask yourself the following questions:
  » Do most of my intuitive experiences come in visual form? That is, in visual imagery and symbolism and flashes?
  » Or do my intuitive experiences tend to come in sounds? Is it a voice I hear?
  » Or do I have a body sensation? A sense of tugging, for example, or a feeling of hot or cold?

This is a useful exercise because, while there are commonalities in intuitive experience, each person recognises and interprets their particular experience in individual ways. Reading other people's stories about intuition in their lives can be helpful, because there are aspects you might relate to, but it is personal practice that will help you locate your own intuition.

Tapping into creative sources

You've got to find the force inside you.
JOSEPH CAMPBELL
AUTHOR AND TEACHER OF COMPARATIVE MYTHOLOGY

Take a few moments to answer the following questions with a 'yes' or a 'no'. Go with your first response, even if you feel the question is complex and requires more careful consideration.

- Do you wish that aspects of your life were different?
- Do you wish you were more creative?
- Is there something you'd like more than anything else in the world?
- Do you find yourself dreaming about living another life?
- Is there anything in your life you'd like to 'fix'?

Most people would answer 'yes' to at least one of these questions, and many would answer 'yes' to all of them. This doesn't necessarily indicate deep unhappiness; rather, it is an indication that a person is yearning for something 'other'.

Your yearning allows you an opportunity to pinpoint what it is that you would like in your life. Often, it is a matter of tapping into creative sources, finding the force that is inside you.

All the exercises in this book will open up paths to these creative sources. Opposite is another exercise that will both tap into your intuitive powers, and give them clues to follow up on.

Exercise — Write away

This exercise involves writing every day, in the morning hours. Try it for a month or two to realise the very real benefits. This is what you do: each morning, when you wake, before you've turned your mind to the day's happenings, to the pulls of duties and deadlines, pick up your pen and write. Simply write.

You may find that what you write comes in the form of questions. It may be phrases or individual words. It may be lists or grievances, praise or musings. As you write, it may seem like nonsense to you, but persevere. Keep going, keep on writing. Give yourself fifteen minutes to get those words on the page, and then stop.

These pages are for you and nobody else. They are a private matter. And the point is not to agonise over them, but to allow whatever is in you to emerge and be given expression. You'll find that rather than spending your days in a mist of unexpressed longings and concerns and wonderings, you'll feel clearer. Over time, you'll find that in that writing will emerge insights and inspirations not usually readily accessible to you.

In writing in this way, your intuitive processes will be stirred and stimulated, and you will find that all sorts of intuitive messages will be revealed. Once you've put down your pen:
- Sit quietly for a few moments.
- Consider any intuitive tugs or flashes that may have emerged.
- Act on them.

What next?

The real voyage of discovery consists not in seeking new landscapes, but in having new eyes.
MARCEL PROUST, AUTHOR

Learning about the wonderful gift of intuition is exciting and expanding. You might feel that there's nothing you can't embark on, nothing you can't have a go at, as long as your faithful friend intuition is right there with you, guiding you and encouraging you.

What can happen, however, is that in time your intuitive powers start to be forgotten:

- Perhaps something difficult happens in your life.
- Perhaps you become so caught up in your day-to-day activities that practising your intuition becomes a low priority.
- You may lose confidence in yourself either because of events, or because your early experiences haunt you.

It is human nature to forget, for any number of reasons. You can take steps, though, that will help you remember to maintain the strength of your intuition. If you decide that your intuition is important enough to you, and valuable enough in your life, you will ensure its continued development.

Here are some suggestions for keeping your intuitive powers burning brightly, for nourishing them so that they feed you in turn, and for deepening your experience of this wonderful gift called intuition.

- Regularly read through this book and follow the exercises described in it. It is by regular practice that you will further develop your intuition, and you'll find that each time you do an exercise, you will have a new outcome.
- Look out for other books, not only on the topic of intuition, but on topics that expand you and help you live life more fully.
- Organise a group to meet and talk about intuition. Share stories about following up on hunches, synchronicities, the benefits of sharpened senses and anything else that allows you to 'grow' your intuition.
- Institute an 'Intuition Day' for yourself. Set aside some time every month or so – it doesn't have to be a whole day, a couple of hours will do – to read through your journal, to add notes to it, and to contemplate how you've used your intuition over the last few weeks. You could also take this opportunity to add to your personal dictionary.

Remember, your intuition will guide you when you feel lost, and give you answers when you thought there were none. It is available to every one of us, and rewards us well for our attention and our listening.

Intuition is a serious business, but it is also fun. Enjoy!